Transported

poems by

Ellen Roberts Young

Finishing Line Press
Georgetown, Kentucky

Transported

Copyright © 2021 by Ellen Roberts Young
ISBN 978-1-64662-420-1 First Edition
All rights reserved under International and Pan-American Copyright Conventions. No part of this book may be reproduced in any manner whatsoever without written permission from the publisher, except in the case of brief quotations embodied in critical articles and reviews.

ACKNOWLEDGMENTS

Unlike my previous chapbooks, these poems developed as a set, one building on or playing off of another. This could make critique difficult. I have been fortunate to participate in two ongoing workshops, Arroyo Writers, who meet monthly, and the Thursday Poets, who meet on first and third Thursday evenings. I've gotten many helpful comments from both groups, and also from two prose writers who are good readers of poetry, Susan Bagby and Joan Glickler.

I thank Joanne Townsend and Leora Zeitlin for their careful reading of the full manuscript.

Publisher: Leah Huete de Maines
Editor: Christen Kincaid
Cover Art: Ellen Roberts Young
Author Photo: Laura C. Puglia
Cover Design: Elizabeth Maines McCleavy

Order online: www.finishinglinepress.com
also available on amazon.com

Author inquiries and mail orders:
Finishing Line Press
PO Box 1626
Georgetown, Kentucky 40324
USA

Table of Contents

Suitcases 1

Beginnings 2

Centripetal Forces 3

Parallel Lines 4

Waiting, September, 1956 5

Greece 7

Transported, October, 1956 8

Unprotected 9

Ground Level 10

Charmed 11

Returns 12

Siblings 14

East and West 15

Il Biciclista 16

Returns II 18

Borrowed Past 20

To Each Their Own 21

Out of the Waters 22

Deep Blue Sea 23

Where I Stand 24

Stone Sentences 25

Accidental 26

*For my brothers, Paul and Scott,
who remember it differently*

Suitcases

We packed a trunk for Egypt,
following lists of "things you can't
easily get there," had it shipped direct,
carried our clothes with us
in thin rectangular suitcases.

Years earlier the British packed trunks
to set up residence in Egypt,
displacing the French. Only a travelling
salesman would carry his own suitcase.

Now every case has wheels,
an expectation of smooth surfaces.

The trunk, shipped home full
of souvenirs—inlaid plates, foot
cushions to be stuffed, kohl bottles—
sits in my bedroom, holding remnants
of childhood, my wedding dress, my
children's art.

Two ceramic geese sit on the green cloth
which covers it like a very low coffee table.
It has shrunk.

Wheeled cases wait in the closet.

Beginnings

Offered a Fulbright, my father chose Egypt
over the Philippines so we could see Europe.
Preparing, Papa read *Mont St. Michel and Chartres,*
Mama read Fodor and phrase books.

We sailed to England, crossed to Paris,
took train to Naples, stepped off another ship
and stumbled over a root of the tree
of "western civilization,"
like stepping through a mirror
and out the other side.

Vines circled the trunk: minarets
alongside pyramids, Arabic and British English.
Sunday tours took us to Giza, Saqqara, Memphis.
We met a people known from tombs
stuffed with the needs of a next life like
the one just left. In Cairo's museum,
stiff statues put their best foot forward,
cases held gold and jeweled pendants,
Tutankhamen's bare bed.

Everywhere mysterious signs. Baffled by
Arabic script I copied the crisp symbols of antiquity:
      n, the running river,
      alef, the vulture
      m, the owl.
Letters I could not weave into words became
ciphers to conjure with. This was the first time
I chose the past over the present

Centripetal Forces

Five lean on each other,
two parents, three children,
no child's star, pointing outward.

Linked like Olympic rings
they learn piastres, lire, share
a rich diet of museums, churches,

operas. Together they enter
the English book store,
stop for mail at American Express.

Mama and Papa study the language,
put children in English-speaking schools.
No classmates come to visit.

The five avoid quarrels, having
only each other, their neighbors strangers.
The children can wander

only on Venice's carless streets,
divide on preferences for
Velazquez or Brueghel.

Returned to a home, a yard, a town
they know, each goes out to friends.
Pressure released, rings unlock,
can't hold the family together.

Parallel Lines

Tales of moats and castles frame
my picture of a king. The Queen
is a prim lady in a trim suit, matching hat.

Alice's nemesis is dwarfed
by the real, living Elizabeth,
her patient smile akin to my mother's,

her age-mate, name-sharer. A child,
I hold these two in equal honor.
My mongrel American family

choosing its tradition, links "English"
and "proper," visits the Cotswolds,
Cambridge, and Windsor Castle,

where neither the Queen nor I can play
with the regal, cased-in-plastic doll house
made for her grandmother, Mary.

Waiting, September 1956

They do not like the separation
but were advised it makes good sense.
They should not risk evacuation,
so all but father stay in Athens.

They were advised it makes good sense—
the British angry over Suez—
if all but father stay in Athens.
The outcome's anybody's guess.

The British angry over Suez,
Egypt laying claim to the canal,
the outcome's anybody's guess.
They should await the all-clear call.

Egypt laying claim to the canal,
mother watches children in the park.
They will await the all-clear call.
To be in Greece and not in school, a lark!

Mother watches children in the park,
buys books, ice cream at four o'clock.
To be in Greece and not in school, a lark,
she takes them to explore the ancient rocks.

Books to read and treats at four o'clock.
The children feel themselves securely moored,
but they begin to tire of ancient rocks;
mother and children both are growing bored.

The children fuss at being safely moored.
Perhaps the talk of danger's overblown.
Mother and children both are growing bored
while father chafes at living all alone.

Thinking the talk of danger's overblown,
they choose to risk evacuation,
both sides chafing at their life alone.
They do not like this separation.

Greece

A school year in Egypt,
most of the next
in Rome, but it was Greece
that grabbed and held me.
In three weeks Athens' high
templed hill, ruined porches
of the Agora, theater of Dionysus,
tucked themselves into memory
like a candle-filled side chapel
that roused my senses
in the cathedral called Europe
so packed with past centuries
it overwhelmed.
                              I left
to become an American teen,
romantic, imagining gold
jewelry, Latin lovers.
Greek stones pulled me back.

Transported, October 1956

Cairo   House at sand's edge   A messenger
Packed trunk in the living room   Wait

Slow convoy, cars without lights   Luggage left
on the pier   My doll held close   His typewriter
Life vests on the deck   Bunk beds
Underwear rinsed out

USS General Patch   Small reunions
Games up and down stairs

Rome   rain
on my 13th birthday: weather like home

Unprotected

We are where we've been: microbes
fed on local air, dust of our early years
are domiciled in the gut, the lungs.
The young mind, porous, expanding,
stores up specifics. Egypt is legless beggars
and giant stone temples, Paris is wide-pathed
gardens, boats on a pond, peanuts
sold to feed pigeons.

At twelve, per Piaget, the mind broadens
to comprehend categories. Young
brains, beginning to build invisibles,
highly susceptible, make use of all
they see—the way a street car
line encircles the city, the distance
between piazzas—to place themselves
on a map still being made.

Adult, I keep my map at hand, add
the new—crooked streets, ornate
facades—to established scaffolding,
only disoriented, enthralled, for a time
(lacking the antibodies locals
have passed down through generations)
until the microbes that sustain me
rise to restore my balance.

Ground Level

Charts tell me it's 2,183 miles
from London to Cairo. Can even crows
fly straight that far? It's where I've been,
what I've seen, a corridor of Europe
from England's monarchy to the Pope's
small independent state, and then beyond.

I ventured east to Vienna, west to Spain,
spent a month in Paris as if it were
a middle ground, bought stamps in small
nations: Liechtenstein, Monaco. All
those crowded countries: no wonder
their people envision splitting into more.

I've travelled much farther on
the sprawling network of U.S. highways,
this country's enormous space. The American
child begins on one block, steps to a store,
grows into notions of space and time
the inverse of Europe's, works back
only to 1492. And then the dinosaurs?

Charmed

A flaunted bracelet:
Eiffel tower, tower of Pisa.
Trajan's column, bridge of sighs.

"I've been there, and there and
there," I could have said, smug
in my poodle skirt and matching
sweaters, chain holding the cardigan.

I could not. I'd have snagged
the sweater, torn the poodle's tail.

And they don't make charms
for dunes or brown rivers,
a steep, wet cobblestone street,

the click of stiletto heels on
terrazzo, or the tiny lizard
in the Villa d'Este garden
hooked to my chain of memory.

Returns

1

She has come home
to the familiar: classmates, neighbors.
Two years older, she doesn't know
what's changed, how corners of her mind
have filled with images foreign to her friends,
dropped in like squash seeds in compost.
She's missed the boy-girl exchanges
of junior high, doesn't know it matters.
High school makes no use of her experience,
her walks among stone ruins and down
art museum halls. Once baring
her forehead because she dreamed
of being a dancer, she switches to bangs,
full skirts, a page boy haircut. Her career
research choice: librarian. As she walks
to Campbell High, not far from her old
grammar school, bookishness defines her
as it did when she was ten.

2

Midway through college she visits
father and brothers in Rome, the city
layered as a self, its past in complex
relation to its present: under,
beside, walked through, lived in.
She walks down narrow ghetto alleys
from the Tiber to Vittorio Emanuele's
"wedding cake," uphill past Trajan's column
to a street of upscale shops. It's a city
for walking as she walked with her father
to the school bus. This summer she
explores with her brothers, studies
Italian, supposes Rome's mix of "my world,
not my world" will be sorted out
on future visits—father settled here,
Campbell left behind.

Siblings

"Ciao" we say, ending each call,
decades after we left Italy together,
after happy separate returns,
after whole years out of touch except
for madonnas on Christmas cards.

Two years apart, often
in separate schools, we ran in the hall,
sparred by the piano. Taken to Europe
we discovered a new world together, differently,
I collecting cheap souvenirs, while you remembered
stories: the catacomb guide who spoke
of oil lamps "for-Christians-to-find-their-way."

We both ate spaghetti al sugo in Trastevere
        inhaled dust lifting from old marble in the Forum
            saw day's light split by stained glass
                in church and cathedral.

Italy lodged inside us, taking a chamber
which might have been Irish, if we
had sampled the ale and explored the ruins
in the County which birthed our ancestors.

East and West

In childhood a trip to the City meant visits
to the zoo, Japanese tea garden, and Chinatown,
with its souvenirs. The West was east
of me. There, heroes on horseback
protected women and children, encouraged
settlements that would have put them
out of business, were the land not too broad
to be truly tamed. For tales not tied to calendars
cameras can film the same rocks for every ambush,
every arrival. In those stories cities
along the Atlantic were dense, inscrutable.

I went east to college; my West moved east
as well. A course on "Western Thought
and Institutions" brought me into Time,
the third dimension lifting story from maps,
lists, into cause and result, origin and end.
"Western history" gave a name to past events
in places I'd visited with my parents,
"Western" the cultural heritage they cherished:
monuments, kings' quarrels, Medieval
Latin and Middle English, Chaucer,
Shakespeare, and Beowulf.

To my father and my professor,
"Western Civilization" meant Europe,
 the source and locus of all their learning,
their degrees, their classes and classifications.
Who was I to question their terms?

Il Biciclista

1

His Irish mother and aunts gave him
no longing for Ireland. His study
of English put England first. Naming cats
James A. Garfield and Chester Arthur showed
his disrespect for cats. He named not one
after an English king, though he could recite
the list by heart, with dramatic pause at
"and so . . . Victoria." Some elder must
have taught him the empire declined
after that great queen's passing.

2

A trip abroad, he feared his only chance,
he'd make the most of it, see England
by bicycle, with family in tow.
He hadn't ridden since his small-town
paper route. Now, his youngest on a seat
at his back, he led his dutiful wife,
his eager older children, from town
to town, over hills and across the fen,
from Frome to Wells, Ely to Cambridge.

3

First England, then the Continent.
Around the curve of years, it was Rome
that turned this son of the countryside, who'd raised
rabbits, chickens, camped among mountain pines,
to a city dweller who knew the bus schedule,
ranked restaurants, stopped each morning
for espresso. He stored a bike for summer
trips, the Italian coast, southern France,
wrote in a tall-shelved study, still a scholar
of English grammar, working to his early end.
Born Catholic fifty years before in San Luis Obispo,
he was buried in Rome's Protestant cemetery.

Returns II

1

With a husband to share it
Greece becomes adventure. They walk
the Acropolis, then go farther,
buy bus tickets, find destinations in letters
she can read but not pronounce, order
food at tavernas by pointing.
She seeks stelae, statues she's studied
in photos in hefty books at the seminar table,
is drawn more to great fluted columns
fallen on ancient pavement, the hidden
stairs at Tiryns, the blue sea below
a high hill on Thassos.
She takes a few photos of her own
for future study, a few of her partner,
expects to return, perhaps to school
in Athens, or, elsewhere around the
Mediterranean, to uncover mosaics
in Tunisia or excavate in Asia Minor.

2

None of the above. Return
to Egypt comes when her children
are about the age she was when she
lived there; she wants them to taste
in a week what she absorbed over months.
Mission work: they hear Arabic prayers
in a protestant church, are taken to visit
a family who have received donated chicks.
Their host blames Copts and Muslims both
for ingrained poverty—their fatalism.
Is it fate that brought her back?
Touring Giza, she meets a visiting scholar
who led tours when she was young.
She has let her own studies drop,
exchanged for church work and activism,
her eyes on the poor, not the Pharaohs.

Borrowed Past

High school made Latin a dull language
of a dull people (too practical: masters
of the arch, they use it to build
aqueducts and sewers.) Greek
was a new script, new syntax
to explore. And it was they
who brought proportion, balance
to Egyptian solidity and made it flow
in garments draping Nike
and the bronze charioteer.

*

Beyond first-year Greek, songs and plays
celebrate legends of wandering warriors,
family quarrels turned deadly:
Achilles, Agamemnon, Oedipus.
Their past becomes my past, as reader
of their texts. Their present: Euclid's
lines and angles expressed in stone
architrave and column, pediments,
friezes. And Thucydides, glorifying
imperial Athens over stubborn Sparta.

*

That present so long past: for a decade
I tried to read a play of Sophocles
or a bit of Aeschylus each summer,
the grand heroes, never went on
to Aristophanes' frogs, birds, wasps.
The candle of youthful delight
in a foreign script that lit my page
had sputtered out.

To Each Their Own

Egyptian gods differ from the frail
humans who wait for Nile's flood,
who embalm hearts and pull
the decomposing brain from the dead.

Fellahin and financiers alike
want a deity with lion's claws and jaw
for protection, one with a jackal's nose
to lead them through death's gate
and out across the sands. Horus,
the hawk, gives the Pharaoh
the wisdom of far-reaching sight.

Greeks, in contrast, ranking humans
high, measure their gods by themselves—
quarrelsome, lusty, proud, possessive
lovers, mothers, fathers. We moderns
build on that base, purify,
disembody, distance the divine.

Animal gods make sense to those
who have not split themselves
from nature. Why shouldn't that cat
be Bastet, summoned to guard the grain?

Out of the Waters

River mothers: Nile,
Tigris, Euphrates.
A great tree sprouted
in their good wet soil, spread
tendrils around the Mediterranean.

The trunk thickens, branches
cover Europe. While settlers
carry seedlings to the Americas,
India, the Pacific, scholars
from England, Germany, France
drift like leaves down to Egypt,
Mesopotamia, and dig, dig. dig.

What's found follows the money,
the conquerors back,
Rosetta Stone to London,
Nefertiti to Berlin,
golden vessels of Ur
to Philadelphia. (Of mummies,
there are enough to go around.)

Seedlings in their different soils
diverge. Those who tend them
contest the claim of Europeans
that theirs is the one true tree.

Deep Blue Sea

From a stony hill on the island Thassos,
this northern thumb of the Mediterranean Sea
      looks as serene a blue as tradition claims.
This sea of Odysseus' wanderings,
      Jonah's big fish, St. Paul's travels,
           this is the sea I picture dropping
      my troubles into, my questions,
my too-extended to-do list,
      rolling water, brilliant blue,
           but salt, no clear lake
      that might reveal what's fallen in.

Mediterranean—between the lands, center
of a triptych—to the north ruins like Pompeii,
      its quickly buried citizens, to the south
the still, bare, ordered rows of
      El Alamein's soldiers; in the middle,
           the never-sated sea, once fed from
      ships like Paul's and Jonah's, now
overfed with bodies fallen
      from overcrowded boats,
           dropped from the cargo
      of refugees carried across its currents.

Where I Stand

In Philadelphia, that once Quaker city,
my seasons of travel drifting into the past,
I take my sons to the Egypt galleries
in Penn's University Museum, show them
mummies, inscribed pillars, fragments
of my childhood fascination.

When museum trips are replaced
by rides to crew practice, my attention
is drawn to news from Central America,
Palestine/Israel, refugees from Sudan—
places I've never been. I stand at protests
at the Federal Building, ride buses to stand
on the Washington Mall. Fridays
I stand with Jewish friends at the Israeli
consulate, sharing bread at 1:00 p.m.
returning next week at 12:00.

This afternoon I walk under trees,
watch sculls on the Schuylkill,
Philadelphia's other, calmer river.
I've seen Cairo's Nile, walked
by Rome's Tiber, discovered
Quaker ancestors who lived
along the Delaware. Native to none
of these, shaped by all, here I stand.

Stone Sentences

Pyramids stripped of their surface survive
thanks to their massive interior stone.

Each damaged monument feeds my desire
for stories of centuries told by cut stone.

Rocks I collect are only on loan:
short-term housing for long-lasting stone.

Since childhood I've found few sights that inspire
me more than the sparkle of sunlight on stone.

My words are unable, however I strive,
to be as definitive as stone.

Ephemeral flesh, impermanent bone
envy the stubborn endurance of stone.

Accidental

Huge stone drums
lie on and around
cracked pavement.
Olympia's Temple of Zeus
is an open platform,
too uneven for dancing.
Do these finely fluted
lifeless things lie
where they fell? Who
can tell us? The guidebook
addresses other pieces
of this intricate puzzle
of change over time.

I, having danced, fallen,
arisen, missed my turn,
am left where I landed,
antique, wreck, beside
the great public square
with its multiple patterns:
donation bricks, pebble
mosaics. Here I sit,
my name not inscribed,
my face not portrayed,
as other dancers
go on to their
next engagement.

After growing up in California (apart from the two years described in this collection) and raising a family in Pennsylvania, **Ellen Roberts Young** became a member of the writing community in Las Cruces, New Mexico in 2004. She has published two chapbooks with Finishing Line Press, *Accidents* (2004) and *The Map of Longing* (2009) as well as individual poems in numerous print and online journals. Her first full-length book of poetry is *Made and Remade* (WordTech Editions, 2014). *Lost in the Greenwood*, a collection focused on Medieval French tapestries, is forthcoming. She is a poetry editor for *Sin Fronteras/ Writers Without Borders Journal* and blogs intermittently at *www.freethoughtandmetaphor.com*.

www.ingramcontent.com/pod-product-compliance
Lightning Source LLC
LaVergne TN
LVHW041517070426
835507LV00012B/1649